Cornerstones of Freedom

The Story of
THE
TRAIL OF TEARS

By R. Conrad Stein

Illustrated by David J. Catrow III

 CHILDRENS PRESS ™

CHICAGO

Library of Congress Cataloging in Publication Data

Stein, R. Conrad.
  The story of the trail of tears.

  (Cornerstones of freedom)
  Includes index.
  Summary: Describes the Federal government's seizure of
Cherokee land in Georgia and the forced migration of the
Cherokee Nation along the Trail of Tears to Oklahoma.
  1. Cherokee Removal, 1838—Juvenile literature.
2. Cherokee Indians—History—Juvenile literature.
[1. Cherokee Removal, 1838. 2. Cherokee Indians—
History. 3. Indians of North America—Southern States—
History] I. Catrow, David J., ill. II. Title.
III. Series.
E99.C5S86   1985   975'.00497   84-28507
  ISBN 0-516-04683-7   AACR2

Campfires flickered and elderly chiefs of various tribes sat cross-legged waiting to hear a speech from the famous Shawnee leader Tecumseh. He had called the council to discuss the survival of the Indian people. "Where today are the Pequot?" Tecumseh asked. "Where are the Narraganset, the Mohican, the Pokanoket, and many other once powerful tribes of our people? They have vanished before the oppression of the white man. . . .Will we let ourselves be destroyed in our turn without a struggle, give up our homes, our country, the graves of our dead, and everything that is dear and sacred to us? I know you will cry with me, 'Never! Never! Never!'"

The gathering of chiefs nodded in agreement. For almost two hundred years, the Indian population had dwindled as the whites pushed steadily westward. White pioneers had a burning thirst for new land, a thirst that seemed unquenchable. Only a strong union among the many tribes would be able to resist their expansion. Tecumseh dreamed of an Indian alliance that would stretch like an iron belt from the Great Lakes to the Floridas and lock the whites into their eastern settlements.

But Tecumseh was killed in battle in 1813. With him died the dream of an Indian united front. No other leader of the time had the diplomatic skills necessary to mold the rival tribes into a confederation powerful enough to withstand the white invasion. Tecumseh's death meant that the white people would face only scattered tribal resistance to their continuing drive into traditional Indian land.

Some of the most desirable Indian land lay in the southeastern United States. Many of the Indians in that region had adopted the white man's ways. Europeans called the Cherokees, Creeks, Choctaws, Chickasaws, and Seminoles the "Five Civilized Tribes" because of their advanced societies.

The most progressive of the Five Civilized Tribes

was the proud Cherokee nation. Years earlier, the Cherokees had dominated a huge territory in the Southeast. A long series of wars and treaties with the whites shrank that area, and by the early 1800s the Cherokees were confined to northern Georgia.

Their land was fertile, however, and the Cherokee nation thrived. Many Cherokees owned small but productive farms. A few owned vast cotton plantations. Still more gathered together and built small towns complete with stores, churches, and schools.

One white missionary, writing in 1808, claimed: "Thus far are the Cherokees advanced; farther I believe than any other nation or tribe in America."

The Cherokees so emulated the whites of the Old South that they even adopted the cruel practice of keeping black slaves. A few Cherokee-owned plantations employed as many as a hundred slaves. Medium-sized farms had between twenty and fifty. Many Cherokee households kept just one or two slaves.

Over the years, many Cherokees married white settlers. Scottish and Irish family names such as Taylor, MacGregor, Lowrey, Smith, McCoy, and Montgomery were common within the tribe. Only full-blooded Cherokees retained traditional Indian names such as Red Eagle or Running Deer.

The desire to educate their youth was almost as powerful as a religious belief among the Cherokees. Tribal leaders were haunted by memories of Indians who had been cheated of their lands because they could not read the treaties they signed. One Cherokee elder, addressing a grade-school class, told the students: "Remember, the whites are near us. . . .Unless you can speak their language and read and write as they do, they will be able to cheat you and trample on your rights. Be diligent therefore in your studies."

Reading was aided by a remarkable alphabet invented by a full-blooded Cherokee named Sequoya. The spoken Cherokee language is a baffling morass of sounds strange to the untrained ear. Getting this complicated language into a form of readily understandable print was an enormous challenge. Working painstakingly with a worn pen, Sequoya tried to put the Cherokee tongue into readable symbols. "It was like catching a wild animal and taming it," he once said. In 1821, after years of effort, Sequoya perfected an alphabet of eighty-six characters. The system was amazingly easy to learn, even for old people who had never been to school. Due to the system's popularity, a Cherokee-language newspaper called the *Cherokee Phoenix* soon circulated everywhere.

The Cherokee government was modeled after the federal government of the United States. It had written laws and the people elected representatives. When dealing with Washington, the government emphasized friendliness and cooperation. The Cherokees refused to join the anti-Washington alliance proposed by Shawnee leader Tecumseh. The

Cherokees even chose to fight alongside white soldiers against their Creek Indian neighbors. During the Creek War of 1812-13, many Cherokees met an ambitious American general named Andrew Jackson. He would later play a crucial role in the fate of the Cherokee people.

Certainly, the Cherokee nation defied the charge that Indians were savages unworthy of land ownership. White settlers often used that argument as an excuse to seize Indian territory. Still, the highly developed Cherokees fell victim to one of the most shameful episodes of injustice ever committed by the government of the United States. They were stripped of the land they so cherished and forced to take a tragic journey later called the Trail of Tears.

In 1828, two events shaped the destiny of the Cherokee nation. First, Andrew Jackson was elected president of the United States. Jackson was known as the champion of the common man. But he was first and last a backwoodsman who boasted that he had been born in a log cabin. Like most pioneers, Jackson carried with him a deeply ingrained hostility toward Indians. He could be kind to individual Indians, but he considered their tribal societies to be savage. Second, gold was discovered

at Dahlonega, Georgia, which was in the heart of Cherokee territory. This development had an immediate and dramatic effect on the Cherokee people.

Gold fever swept the South. Miners, hungry for a quick fortune, invaded the Cherokee nation. Many of the miners stole Indian cattle and attacked Indian women. Neighboring whites, who coveted Cherokee land, encouraged the miners. Hoping to harass the Indians into giving up their territory, the whites organized groups called Pony Clubs. These were gangs of rowdies who rode into Cherokee country to start fires and plunder homes.

Many young Cherokees wanted to fight the white invaders. But the older men knew that any act of violence on the part of the Indians would give the state government and President Jackson the excuse they needed to send soldiers marching onto their land. Writing in the *Cherokee Phoenix,* one leader said: "It has been the desire of our enemies that the Cherokees may be urged to some desperate act. Thus far, this desire has never been realized, and we hope...this forbearance will continue."

Vowing not to fight, the Cherokee people demonstrated their degree of civilization by taking their grievances to court. They argued that the federal government had granted them their land by treaty and therefore they should be protected from the gold miners, from their greedy neighbors, and from the government of the state of Georgia, which also wanted their lands. The Georgia court gave the Cherokees no help at all. Governor George Gilmer summed up his feelings about land treaties with Indians in this statement: "Treaties were expedients by which ignorant, intractable, and savage people were induced without bloodshed to yield up what civilized peoples had a right to possess."

Eventually, a Cherokee lawsuit reached the

United States Supreme Court, the highest court in the land. After a series of decisions, the court ruled in 1832 that the federal government must protect the Cherokee nation from its many intruders. But only the president of the United States had the authority to send troops to ward off the invaders of Cherokee land. At the time, President Jackson was preparing for his second term. He refused to help Indians in a conflict against whites. Also, Supreme Court Justice John Marshall was his political enemy. In a historic defiance of the Supreme Court's authority, President Jackson proclaimed, "John Marshall has rendered his decision; now let him enforce it."

Moreover, President Jackson considered even harsher methods of dealing with Indians. For almost three decades, government leaders had discussed a plan called Indian Removal. The plan was as simple as it was devilish. It called for the removal, by force if necessary, of all Indians east of the Mississippi. The Indians were to be resettled on land west of the river. Actually, this form of migration had been going on for generations. Many northern tribes had already quietly retreated westward in order to avoid further conflicts with the whites. But in the

John Marshall

Andrew Jackson

South, the Five Civilized Tribes clung tenaciously to their territories while white frontiersmen demanded their removal.

Raising the question of Indian Removal, President Jackson told Congress: "I suggest for your consideration the propriety of setting apart an ample district west of the Mississippi. . .to be guaranteed to the Indian tribes as long as they shall occupy it . . . ." Jackson's pioneer supporters cheered his every word. Under his leadership, the Indian Removal Act became the law of the land.

A feeling of gloom hung like a stubborn fog over the Cherokee nation. Many people simply could not believe that the Indian Removal Act had actually passed Congress. The Cherokee land had been given to the tribe by a treaty endorsed by the federal government. Cherokee people had lived there for countless generations before the coming of the whites. Also, the Cherokees were a community of farmers, not nomadic hunters who could pack up and move at the government's decree.

A debate raged among tribal leaders. One leader, John Ross, wanted to fight removal through the courts. Another, the elderly Major Ridge, urged the people to move to the West because he felt that President Jackson's position was unshakeable. Hundreds of Cherokee families made plans to hide in caves in the remote hills. Others simply gave up and trekked to the West before they were ordered to do so.

Meanwhile, Georgia authorities and the land-hungry white frontiersmen lay like vultures outside the Cherokee boundaries. Even while the many cases were being argued in court, the state of Georgia organized a lottery to distribute Cherokee land. Lucky winners were given 160-acre farms or 40-acre mining sites, all to be parceled out just as soon as the Indians were forced off their territory. A popular song of the time began with the words:

> All I want in this creation
> Is a pretty little wife and a big plantation
> Way down yonder in the Cherokee Nation.

In other parts of the South, the Indian Removal
Act crushed the Five Civilized Tribes. During the
bitter winter of 1831, the migration of the Choctaws
began. Many were barefoot and most had no coats or
blankets. Yet they were forced to cross the
Mississippi River in zero-degree weather. The
federal government had agreed to feed and clothe
the Indians during their journey, but money for the

provisions was never sent. The Creeks were driven out of their homes in 1836. The unwilling Creeks were put in chains and marched double file by United States soldiers. Some thirty-five hundred Creeks who started the trek died of hunger and exposure before they reached their new territory. In 1837, the Chickasaws loaded their belongings into wagons and began their sad journey westward. Only the Seminoles chose to fight. However, after a long and bloody war, most members of that tribe were herded to the West also.

By battling through the courts, the Cherokee people resisted migration until 1838. Then the federal government acted on a treaty agreement that was yet another sad chapter in the story of the Trail of Tears. The treaty agreement, concluded two years earlier, gave away all Cherokee lands east of the Mississippi in exchange for new lands in the West and a cash settlement. But the agreement was signed by only a tiny minority of the Cherokee people. Some of the signers had been bribed by government officials. Still, the federal government insisted that the treaty was valid.

The month of May, 1838, was the beginning of a long nightmare for the Cherokee people. General Winfield Scott, who would later run for president, led an army of seven thousand troops into Cherokee territory—nearly one soldier for every two Cherokees. Without warning, the troops burst into Cherokee homes, dragged the people outside, and drove them toward staging camps. Anyone moving too slowly was prodded by a soldier's bayonet.

Following almost on the heels of the soldiers came

neighboring whites who swept up the Cherokees' personal possessions just as soon as the soldiers had forced the Indians from their homes. Like pirates, the whites stuffed sacks with pots, pans, silverware, and musical instruments, all looted from Cherokee houses and cabins. Fist fights, knife fights, and pistol duels broke out over the booty. Some of the whites, knowing that the Indians often buried their dead with gold and silver jewelry, dug up graves and sifted through decaying corpses searching for treasure.

On June 16, 1838, a Baptist minister named Evan Jones reported: "The Cherokees are nearly all prisoners. They had been dragged from their houses and encamped at the forts and military places, all over the nation. Multitudes were allowed no time to take anything with them except the clothes they had on. Females. . .are driven on foot before the bayonets of brutal men. . . .It is the work of war in time of peace."

Dismayed and disbelieving, the Cherokees wandered about the camps as if in a daze. Many of the white troops who guarded the Indians felt shamed by their duties. "I [later] fought through the War between the States," wrote one infantryman, "and I saw men shot to pieces by the thousands, but the Cherokee Removal was the cruelest work I ever knew."

The staging camps held an estimated seventeen thousand Cherokees. They included sick people, crippled people, elderly men and women, crying babies, and children. Some were put on riverboats for the trip west. Others were led away from the camps in small parties. But the majority of the tribe made the long, bitter walk together in a journey they called *Nunna-da-ul-tsun-yi*. In the Cherokee language this meant, "The Place Where They Cried." History would forever afterward call the trek the Trail of Tears.

On a June morning, a long, ragged column of Cherokees began their westward march. Some of the Indians rode horses or wagons, but the majority walked. A Cherokee named William Coodey later wrote: "Groups of persons formed about each wagon. The day was bright and beautiful, but a gloomy thoughtfulness was depicted in the lineaments of every face....[Suddenly] a low sound of distant thunder fell on my ears....A dark spiral cloud was rising above the horizon and sent forth a murmur [like] a voice of divine indignation for the wrong of my poor and unhappy countrymen, driven by brutal power from all they loved and cherished in the land of their fathers. . . ."

Behind the Cherokees spread the red Georgia clay and the land they had known for generations. Ahead lay an area in present-day Oklahoma that the people had never seen before. The government called the area "Indian Territory." In between stretched almost a thousand miles of forests, mountains, swamps, and tortuous wilderness roads.

Every day the sun raged like a branding iron in the heavens. The countryside suffered from drought. The Cherokees prayed for rain, but none came. Streams and creeks dried to sand, and the people's throats burned with thirst. Still they marched. And every step took them farther away from their homeland.

Diseases such as measles and whooping cough spread from one marcher to another. Frontier whites who saw the once proud Cherokee nation pass sadly in front of their homes wrote their relatives back East: "The poor people. They are dying like flies."

Winter struck. It was as cold and forbidding as the summer had been broiling. A howling wind

engulfed the people in snow and sleet. A traveler from the state of Maine passed a Cherokee camp and wrote home: "Aging females, apparently nearly ready to drop into the grave, were traveling with heavy burdens attached to their backs—on the frozen ground with no covering for their feet except what nature had given them. We learned from the inhabitants on the road where the Indians passed that they buried fourteen or fifteen at each stopping place."

It took more than six months for all the people to travel the full length of the Trail of Tears and reach Oklahoma. It is estimated that one of every four of the Cherokees who started the long march from Georgia died along the route.

The tragedy of the journey can be appreciated in the broken English of a full-blooded Cherokee man who years later spoke to a historian: "Long time we travel on way to new land. People feel bad when they leave old nation. Womens cry and make sad wails. Children cry and many men cry, and all look sad when friends die, but they say nothing and just put heads down and keep on go towards West. Many days pass and people die very much. We bury close by trail."

The heartbreak of the Cherokees did not end with the Trail of Tears. The federal government had granted the Cherokees and the other Indian tribes their land in Oklahoma for "as long as the grass shall grow and the streams shall run." But just a scant few years after the Indians were resettled, white pioneers began to probe into their territory. The federal government did little to discourage them. After the Civil War, the white invaders became a horde. Parcel by parcel, the federal government bought up or seized Indian territory and opened it officially to white farmers. By the turn of the century, the Indian nations in Oklahoma held almost no land at all.

In Georgia, the Cherokee people had not been completely eradicated. A few hundred Cherokees avoided General Scott's roundup by hiding in the hills. One of them, a man named Tsali, became a legend. Even today, the Cherokees tell his story.

Tsali killed a white soldier after he saw that soldier jabbing a bayonet at Tsali's wife. General Scott, the officer in charge, knew it would be difficult to capture Tsali and to flush out the hundreds of other Cherokees who resisted migration by living in caves. So Scott sent word to Tsali that if

he would give himself up, the army would abandon
its efforts to find other Indians hiding in the hills.
Tsali agreed to the terms and surrendered to Scott.
He was sentenced to death for killing the soldier.

On a warm summer morning, Tsali faced a firing
squad. As a final act of cruelty, the army forced
Cherokee prisoners to serve as his executioners.
Tsali refused a blindfold. Instead, he spent his final
instant on this earth gazing at the red clay of the old
Cherokee nation. It is said his last words were, "It is
sweet to die in one's own country."

About the Author

R. Conrad Stein was born and grew up in Chicago. He enlisted in the Marine Corps at the age of eighteen and served for three years. He then attended the University of Illinois where he received a bachelor's degree in history. He later studied in Mexico, earning an advanced degree from the University of Guanajuato. Mr. Stein is the author of many other books, articles, and short stories written for young people.

Mr. Stein now lives in Chicago with his wife, Deborah Kent, who is also a writer of books for young readers, and their daughter Janna.

About the Artist

David J. Catrow III was born in Virginia and grew up in Hudson, Ohio. He spent three years in the United States Navy as a hospital corpsman then subsequently attended Kent State University, where he majored in biology. He is a self-taught illustrator. Mr. Catrow currently lives in Hudson, Ohio with his wife Deborah Ann and daughter Hillary Elizabeth. The artist would like to thank Deborah for her constant support and inspiration.